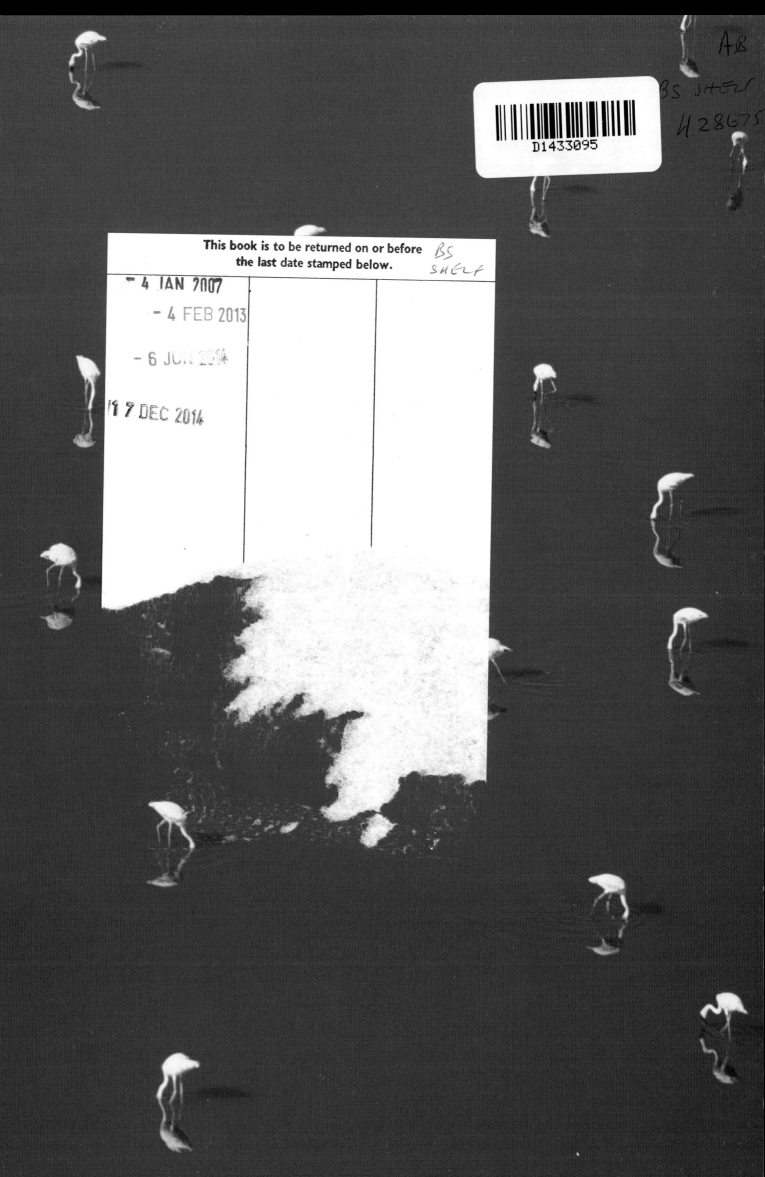

Untamed

Animals Around the World

Untamed
Animals Around the World

Photographs by
Steve Bloom

Text by
Christian Havard

Illustrations by
Emmanuelle Zicot

HARRY N. ABRAMS, INC., PUBLISHERS

CONTENTS

In the Water

Sleeping

Feeding

The Rhythm of the Seasons

Life in Extreme Conditions

Endangered Species

Photographing the Animal World

While holidaying in South Africa, photographer Steve Bloom developed an interest in animals—like any other tourist, he took his camera on safari. This trip, however, was to alter his whole life and, on his return to England, he decided to become a wildlife photographer. Then, watching the behaviour of a gorilla in a zoo, he began to wonder what sort of life great apes lead in the wild—a reflection which set him travelling round the globe to meet them in their natural environments.

After two years photographing primates like the gorilla, orang-utan, and the chimpanzee, he began to take an interest in other animals. Although Steve travels to many countries, Africa is the place he loves most: hardly surprising since this is where he was born and raised.

What is most astonishing about Steve's photographs is the impression of closeness: you feel you could almost touch the animals. But, ever prudent, Steve only approaches those accustomed to meeting human beings. For the more dangerous creatures, he uses a camera with high-powered telescopic lenses. Every situation, however, is unique, and he constantly has to adapt. He photographs lions from his car, using it as a shield. When approaching grizzly bears in Alaska—they hate being surprised—he talks loudly and continuously to warn them he's coming: if he tried to creep up on them, the bears might react violently and attack. In spite of all these precautions, Steve has been

in some seriously scary situations. In India, he was perched on the back of a vehicle photographing rhinos when one of them suddenly charged. There was no time to take evasive action but, fortunately, the animal changed course at the last moment and the occupants escaped unharmed.

A quality essential to the photographer's art is patience. Steve decided, against all odds, to try and capture on camera a great white shark leaping out of the water. He spent more than 15 days on a small boat, his eye glued to the viewfinder, roasting in the fierce sun and his stomach churning with seasickness, before he finally got his chance. Even under such arduous conditions, Steve managed to catch this magnificent spectacle—a spectacle lasting only a second or two.

There are other animals dear to Steve Bloom—endangered species, such as pandas and Siberian tigers. Because so very few remain in the wild, it's a rare event indeed to photograph them there. So Steve goes to China to visit wildlife parks that attempt to reproduce these creatures' natural environment, protecting them and preventing their total disappearance.

Photographing wildlife is a wonderful way to make a living, a privilege in fact, with each day bringing its crop of surprises. But over and above Steve's passion for photography and animals is the challenge of making the whole world aware of the dire situation of so many species.

On foot and in the air

In the forests of Madagascar, *Verreaux's sifaka* sometimes travels on its hind legs. The *leopard* shown here is about to spring up a tree to look for prey.

Animals travel around—on foot or by air—to hunt for food, adjust to the changing seasons by migration, escape enemies, move house or win new territory.

The world of animals is wonderfully complex—a universal ballet with a cast of creatures endlessly running, soaring, fleeing, whirling, skating, swimming. If they stop moving, it's to watch for prey—like the leopard lying in ambush—or to hide from a predator, rest or bask in the sun, protect themselves from the cold and wind, or sleep. They also go to ground to give birth or hatch their eggs: to bring forth new life, little bundles of energy like this baby *Verreaux's sifaka* clinging to its mother's back.

All land mammals walk on four feet, and hence are called quadrupeds. The only exception is man, who is a biped. When they leave the trees to travel on the ground, some of the larger apes (the *gorilla* and *chimpanzee*) and lemurs (the *sifaka* and *ringtail*) also walk upright.

Most birds fly, but some are flightless (ratites), such as the *ostrich* and the *rhea*.

The *okapi*, a Congolese cousin of the *giraffe*, walks by raising both feet on one side of its body at the same time. This type of gait is known as 'ambling'.

Speed and Endurance

The *cheetah* is the fastest of the cats. Over a short distance (a few dozen metres or so), it can reach 110 km/h. The *white rhinoceros* is somewhat less agile—it has to shift 1,500 to 3,000 kg! But it still manages almost 50 km/h.

The *white rhinoceros* seldom travels very far. In one day it will trot only 10 to 20 km between its grazing grounds, the water-holes it drinks from and the mud baths where it wallows to gain protection from the heat.

The *cheetah*, too, doesn't move around much as there's enough prey in its immediate surroundings. On the other hand, catching it is never easy. Even if it gets as close as possible to its victims, they can run fast as well. For example, the *impala* can do 75 km/h, with bounds 10 m long and 3 m high! Eight times out of ten it manages to escape. The cheetah is, in fact, a sprinter: it runs fast but is soon exhausted. It then takes a long time to recover.

The animal world also has its marathon specialists: the *elephant*, the *wolf*, the *reindeer*. The reason they wander, however, is always the same: the search for food.

The *elephant* lives in herds and its appetite is enormous: it eats between 150 and 250 kg of grass and leaves a day, depending on the season. If the herd were to stay in the same place, it would quickly consume all available food. So it travels hundreds of kilometres, always taking the same route, before returning to its point of departure…and then setting off again. These migrations result in careful husbanding of resources, with the vegetation able to re-grow during the herd's absences.

The *wolf* can run for long distances without tiring. It can trot at about 20 km/h, with top speeds of 50 km/h in deep snow on the wide open spaces of Canada.

In the Water

The Camargue is the realm of bulls, birds, horses…
and water. The magnificent, semi-wild members of the
horse family run freely among the salt marshes and the
countless streams.

At birth, the *Camargue foal* is completely black. As it grows it turns grey and on reaching adulthood acquires its permanent white coat. Water is these horses' playground, but they share this with the region's bulls and a huge variety of birds: the *little egret*, the *pink flamingo* and the *marsh harrier*, for instance. And if the water in a channel is too deep to wade, it doesn't matter: this horse is an excellent swimmer and nothing can stand in the way of its freedom.

Most mammals can swim naturally, with the exception of the great apes. The *orang-utan* sometimes visits a pond or a watercourse to nibble a few aquatic plants, but it merely stands in the water, close to the bank, sometimes hanging on to a branch with one hand.

Some animals are totally dependent on the aquatic environment. The *hippopotamus* (a cousin of the horse) spends the whole day in the water to protect its delicate skin from the African sun. It rests and swims and walks on the bottom—not at all bothered by its weight of 1.5 to 2.5 tonnes. It's in the water that the big males challenge each other for the favour of the females. They also reproduce in the water. They wait for the sun to go down before clambering on to the land to graze the grass.

The Camargue is also a paradise for the *pink flamingo*. With its curious curved beak, it filters the water for small shellfish, larvae and algae.

Animal Acrobats

Leaping from branch to branch is the preferred mode of travel for most monkeys—as well as their favourite game. In the jungles of Borneo, a mother *proboscis monkey*, her baby clinging to her belly, launches herself into the air to reach another tree.

The conquest of the skies! This is the wonderful heritage of birds. They are the only creatures with wings and so we think of them as the only ones that can fly. In fact, that's not quite true. They have to share the kingdom of the air with a few very special mammals.

The best known of these mammals and the true 'fliers' are the *bats*. The membrane that connects the long fingers on their hands, their hind legs and their tails serves as a wing. Most bats are nocturnal and therefore specialists in night flying. They swirl around chasing after insects using an ultrasound system known as 'echolocation': on encountering a target, the sound wave created by their cries bounces back to them as an echo.

Other mammals, such as *flying squirrels*, are actually gliders. The skin stretched between their legs and bellies (the *patagium*) enables them to travel several tens of metres when they launch themselves into the air from tree to tree.

As for the *monkeys*, most are the acrobats of the high treetops. Thanks to their hands and tails, they can latch on to the smallest branch to perform their aerial gymnastics. Every leap is calculated: there's no question of missing the intended branch as a fall could be fatal.

Moving around like this is also, for such monkeys as the *proboscis*, a way of avoiding having to climb down to the ground, where they could expose themselves to predators.

The Antarctic cold and storms hold no terror for the *wandering albatross*. With its 3-metre wing span, it often takes advantage of air currents to glide and rest its wings.

Private Property!

The *bald eagle* is an ace acrobat. Looping the loop, flying on its back, pirouetting—the eagle executes the most complicated manoeuvres to make life difficult for rivals.

In the animal kingdom, very little is done on a whim; rather, everything is based on instinct: eating (and avoiding being eaten), sleeping and the perpetuation of the species. To achieve these three objectives, animals must first find the most suitable habitat: a space they can conquer and defend—what we call their territory.

In the breeding season, perched on a big tree close to its nest, the *bald eagle* keeps watch over its territory. It will defend this by force if necessary against any other eagle that tries to take it. No trespassers are permitted: the female is sitting on her eggs and mustn't be disturbed. Nor can other eagles nest too close. If they did, there wouldn't be enough prey to go round when the young are born. If a fight breaks out, screams and threatening flight manoeuvres are usually enough to frighten off interlopers.

Animals that live on the ground behave in much the same way but frequently they also mark their territory. Thus *wolves* in a pack regularly patrol the perimeter of their territory, where they leave droppings or spray with urine. Other packs are thus warned to keep their distance. If any pack ignores this boundary and hunts in the other's area, a battle will ensue. Again, though, there aren't many violent clashes, and the weaker animals will soon give way to the stronger.

In a *herring gull* colony, territory is divided very simply. It's just a matter of keeping out of reach of your neighbour's beak when you're sitting on your nest.

Dominance and Social Status

Beware boxing kangaroos! Actually, kangaroos don't box—this is just a myth created by humans. In the violent close-quarter fighting observed between *grey kangaroos* the terrific blows these animals inflict on their opponents' stomachs are produced with the hind legs.

Among polygamous species, the male must acquire as many females as possible. He must then hang on to them by forming a harem which he watches over and protects from his rivals.

In the semi-desert plains of the Australian outback, the *grey kangaroo* lives in small family groups, or 'mobs' consisting of one male, two or three females and the three or four youngest offspring. The females are very fertile and capable of raising three differently aged young simultaneously: a baby at a nipple, a joey in mother's pouch and a bigger one at her side. The young males are always ready to take the place of the dominant males—hence the frequent confrontations. In spite of their powerful kick, a fight is never fatal and ceases as soon as one opponent realises his inferiority and retreats.

The outback is also the domain of the *dingo*, a small wild dog (between 15 and 20 kg in weight and 40–50 cm tall) which lives in a dispersed pack. This pack comprises several families and some lone animals. They all defend the territory, and big prey (*grey* and *red kangaroos*) are hunted by the whole pack. Young males and females regularly leave the pack to join another group. This prevents interbreeding and introduces fresh blood to the various families.

The Australian desert is the last place in the world where flocks of wild *dromedaries* can be found. Sadly, even here their numbers are declining.

Peaceful Conquest

The *red-crowned crane*, known in Japan as the 'Goddess of the Marshes', was designated an 'outstanding natural monument' by the Japanese authorities in 1952. At that time there were only about thirty left. The species is now fully protected and, today, their numbers have increased to around a thousand.

The heart of a beautiful female can be won by dancing. *Red-crowned cranes* gather on the marshes in winter to perform their courtship rituals. In pairs, beaks gaping and wings spread, the birds do battle with leaps, bows and rhythmic steps. They toss grass and twigs into the air while emitting loud, trumpet-like cries. Once mated, a pair bonds for life. And they continue to dance for each other, all year round.

Another great performer is to be found in the massif of the Vosges: the *Western Capercaillie*. Year after year and in the same place, the males gather to dance. Solemnly singing, plumage a-shimmer and throats swelling, they squabble with flapping wings as they confront each other under the apparently indifferent gaze of the females. Yet those bored hens will choose the lucky victor when the display is over. The cock, however, is pretty fickle. After mating with the first hen, he'll come back and dance again to make another conquest.

Some birds even offer their partners a present to seduce them: a pebble or a twig for the nest. To show off his fishing skills, the *cormorant* presents his chosen mate with a gift of a fish.

His tail spread like a fan and beak raised, the *blue-footed booby* dances by lifting his big, webbed feet high in the air.

Conquest by Force

The *tiger* will not tolerate any other males on his territory—only females. So when a rival crosses his border, a fight is inevitable: there's not enough space for the two of them.

In the wild, it's common for males to fight over females. These confrontations are ritualised: threatening postures, possibly a fight followed by the retreat of the weaker male. The death of one of the combatants is rare, and always the result of an accident. A deep scratch may, for example, result in an infection and, hence the death of a *tiger*. Similarly, two *stags* may get their antlers entangled and die of starvation, unable to extricate themselves. *Walrus* battles have a reputation for ferocity—a male may be ripped open by a tusk and succumb to his injuries.

The *orang-utan's* behaviour is not exactly gentlemanly. A male doesn't fight with males, but females. If a female ventures on to his territory, he forces her to mate with him in order to pass on his own genes.

But the fiercest creature, in terms of winning a mate, is the bird chosen as a symbol of peace: the *dove*. Sometimes the stronger male will pursue his adversary as he flies away; if he catches him, he'll have no qualms about beating him to death!

The female *praying mantis* has the charming habit of devouring the male after mating. She performs this cannibalistic act because she needs an immediate source of protein if her body is to manufacture eggs.

Who's the Lucky One?

The *scarlet macaw* (or *Ara macao*) originates from South America. It lives in family groups in forests of very tall, sparse trees. Like all parrots, however, it's under threat from the trade in tropical birds.

In the bird kingdom, it's the female who chooses her partner. The lucky male will be the one with the handsomest plumage or the finest song, or who can make the cosiest nest. All these qualities are signs that a creature's in good health and therefore most likely to produce robust offspring.

All *scarlet macaws* have identically coloured plumage. So when choosing her mate, the female will base her decision on the quality and length of the male's feathers and his cries. Hard luck, therefore, on anyone who's spoiled his feathers, got parasites or 'lost' his voice—he's got no chance! The couples that result are very closely bonded and pair for life.

The male *peacock* is a regular Casanova. He has 150 long, highly developed feathers on his back, often wrongly thought to be tail feathers. To draw attention to himself, he extends these feathers like a fan and sets them quivering. He folds his wings, lifts his tail and struts around the females. The females watch this display and then choose the best-looking male. Sometimes a small group of females will form around a male whilst he mates several times with each of them.

This female *hamadryas baboon* is displaying her scarlet rump to show she's ready to mate.

Family Life

Lions live in family groups composed of lionesses, their cubs and one or two dominant males. After three and a half months of gestation, the lioness produces three or four young. She lives alone with her cubs for a few weeks before rejoining the pride.

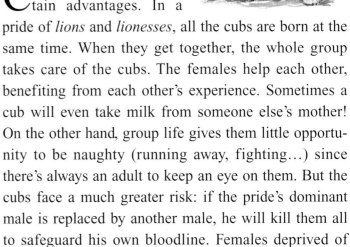

Communal life has certain advantages. In a pride of *lions* and *lionesses*, all the cubs are born at the same time. When they get together, the whole group takes care of the cubs. The females help each other, benefiting from each other's experience. Sometimes a cub will even take milk from someone else's mother! On the other hand, group life gives them little opportunity to be naughty (running away, fighting…) since there's always an adult to keep an eye on them. But the cubs face a much greater risk: if the pride's dominant male is replaced by another male, he will kill them all to safeguard his own bloodline. Females deprived of their young in this way will immediately come on heat ready to produce more cubs.

Far from the African savannah, on the high plateaux of the Andes, the *vicuna* (a cousin of the llama) brings just one kid into the harem. As soon as it's born it tries to stand up. After half an hour or so of repeated struggles and falls, it finally staggers to the comforting teats of its mother. An hour later it's galloping and cavorting round her. Like the lion cubs, the baby is made welcome by all the mothers, and it quickly joins in exploring and playing with other young herd members.

The wild *rabbit* may have from one to seven litters of between three and twelve young a year—which makes an average of four litters of five young a year, or twenty babies!

Single Mothers

Springtime. In a flooded meadow, *bear cubs* trot after their mother. She's anxious to reach cover: even for powerful animals like these, walking in the open is always dangerous. Even more caution is essential with young around.

A mother's life is not an easy one: most males leave their partners after mating so the females must bring up their young and protect them on their own. The *bear* brings one to three cubs into the world in a well-concealed den—often a cave with an entrance screened by bushes.

The little bear cub weighs scarcely 500 g at birth, its eyes are closed and it's virtually naked. It will stay in the den with its mother for almost four months before venturing outside. Although weaned at 18 months, it won't be independent until it's two or three. When accompanied by her young, the female is careful to avoid meeting males because their reactions are unpredictable and they may attack small cubs.

But not all fathers are like the bear. On the plains of North America, the *coyote* is a model father. When the arrival of his offspring is imminent, he hunts alone to bring the female food as she waits to give birth in the burrow they've chosen together. When the babies are born, he helps groom them with energetic licking. He guards the entrance to the den and keeps intruders out. When the young begin to eat meat, he brings them their first prey and, later, teaches them how to hunt for themselves.

Beaks agape, these *robin chicks* await their next mouthful. Their parents take turns to feed them all day long.

Bringing Up Baby

A mother *orang-utan* full of tenderness and affection for her baby. She suckles it for three to four years before contemplating a new birth. If all goes well, she'll have an average of five babies during her lifetime.

Bringing up the young is the work of either the mother alone or both parents. Once that period of upbringing is over and the young have grown up, they are often forcibly ejected from the family home by their parents, who are preparing for new births. The youngsters must now fend for themselves, with no hope of ever rejoining their family.

A mother *orang-utan* looks after her baby by herself, and it's by watching its mother that the youngster learns. Very quickly she teaches her baby how to swing on a vine, how to walk and how to leap among the trees. She shows it how to distinguish leaves and fruit that are good to eat from those that are poisonous. By protecting herself, the mother instructs her baby about the dangers of its environment: predators, for instance, or dangerous actions like uncontrolled leaps. And when the time comes for them to part, with the youngster some five or six years old, she will drive it out…for good.

The female *cuckoo* is the most ruthless of creatures: she forces a couple of strangers to foster her child. She has the nasty habit of laying her eggs in the nest of another bird, such as a *dunnock* or *warbler*. When the baby cuckoo hatches, it immediately tosses the other eggs out of the nest—or even the chicks if they were hatched first! Once it's on its own, its adoptive parents will have to keep on feeding it, even if it turns out to be five times their size!

A young *Eleonora's falcon* hesitates before launching itself into the void. After 40 days in the nest, the great moment has arrived for its first flight.

Protecting the Little Ones

When in a hurry, a *lioness* will pick up her young cub by the scruff, carrying it unharmed in her mouth. The *elephant cow* always keeps one eye on her calf to ensure it's close by her side.

Whatever their species, all babies are fragile and vulnerable. There's always a predator waiting to take advantage of a moment's distraction on the part of the parents and carry off a young one to devour it. So every animal has developed strategies to protect its offspring as best it can.

Elephant calves faced with danger take refuge between the legs of the adults. On the icy tundra of the Arctic, young *musk oxen* do the same when the *white wolf* attacks. But the *wolf* has his work cut out; as soon as the pack is spotted, the *musk oxen* form a circle, with their heads facing outward. The young must then take refuge behind the adults, where they'll be safe. The wolves find themselves confronted by a solid barrier of huge, pointed horns; only by force of numbers and cunning do they sometimes manage to break through and carry off a young calf.

When their mother goes off hunting, young *leopards* are also in danger. Still too small to accompany her, they lay up in thickets or in a hole. But *hyenas* are always on the prowl and sometimes find out where they're hiding. Hyenas show no mercy: they carry them off and eat them. One of the mother *leopard's* tricks is to move her young regularly, carrying them in her mouth from one hiding place to another.

These *fox* cubs are playing in the grass under their mother's watchful eye. At the slightest sign of danger, the whole family runs and hides in the den.

Lessons for Life

This young *grizzly bear* is trying to catch gulls as they swoop over the riverbank. As yet, he lacks experience.

Young animals play to test their abilities, establish a pecking order and learn the lessons of life.

A young *fawn* joins the herd of *does* one or two weeks after birth. There it meets other young *deer*. Playing allows them to hone their skills as they chase after each other, cavorting all over the meadows. The bigger they grow, the further away from the females their games take them. This way they gradually distance themselves from their mothers and learn to be independent.

Through play, especially mock fights, young *bear* cubs learn who's the strongest or bravest. When they climb trees there's always one who goes higher than all the rest or ventures out along a thin branch. Playing improves your agility and, above all, teaches you how to assess risks: the cubs must learn not to fall.

It may seem like a cruel game to us when cats play with their prey before eating it. *Lynx* cubs, for instance, do this when their parents bring them a live *field mouse*. The youngsters amuse themselves letting it go and catching it time and again; they prod it and bat it around with their paws before turning it into a meal. In fact, it's not a game but the way cubs practise their hunting skills.

Lion cubs use the adults as their playground, grabbing their tail tufts, pulling their ears and climbing on Daddy's back—the fun is endless!

Adults Play, Too

Sheltered in her lair and after a hibernation lasting several months, the mother polar bear gives birth in January to two cubs. The babies divide their time between playing and resting.

It's not only young animals who play. Adults do too, with their young or among themselves, for the sheer pleasure of it.

Even though *polar bears* live alone (the male on his own and the female with her young), encounters do take place on the ice floes. After the customary formalities establishing dominance—who has to give way to whom—the bears take a short break to relax. Then the mock fights begin, the slides and 'dance routines' that briefly enliven the vast white desert. When all is over, each bear goes its own way again.

The *wolf* is a bit of a joker: it hides behind a rock or a bush and waits for another member of the pack to pass by, then jumps out on him. A battle follows, but a friendly one, which the two *wolves* thoroughly enjoy. Indeed, they're often joined by other pack members, and the scuffle quickly turns into one great big, happy, free-for-all.

And then there are the *crows*, an impressive sight swirling, pirouetting, diving. They wheel on their backs, singly or in groups, cawing raucously. Some have even been spotted repeatedly 'skating' on frozen lakes or down the slopes of snow-covered roofs.

The *otter* uses the riverbanks like a toboggan run. It slides into the water on its back or tummy, then climbs up the bank and starts all over again!

Marine Mammals

The *bottlenose dolphin* lives in groups called schools in tropical and temperate seas. This excellent swimmer can reach speeds of 50 km/h—no mean feat for a giant measuring up to 4 m in length and with a maximum weight of 500 kg!

Contrary to what some people think, whales, seals and dolphins are not fish: they are marine mammals. Hence they have to surface regularly to breathe (they have lungs, not gills) and, like all mammals, they suckle their young.

In France, at low tide in the Somme Estuary, you'll see groups of twenty or so young seal cubs lying asleep, stretched out on the sand banks. When the tide rises and tickles their tummies, they swim out to sea to hunt. They consume only 2–3 kg of crustaceans and small fish a day, despite their body weight of between 50 and 130 kg.

Baby seals are born at the beginning of July. On the sand, the pup, or baby seal, sucks at its mother's two teats for one minute every four hours for about three to five months. From birth it can stay underwater for two minutes, then later for up to ten, before it needs to surface for air.

Unlike the seal, the dolphin gives birth and suckles her young—for one year—in the water. Her two teats are located at the base of her belly. An adult dolphin can remain submerged without breathing for some eight minutes, diving to a depth of 250 m.

With its horse's head, fat belly and lizard-like tail, the *sea-horse* must be one of the strangest-looking fish! Also strange is that it is the father, not the mother, who looks after the young.

Deep Sea Sailors

The *humpback whale* is a member of the Cetacean family. It has no teeth but 'baleens', or bony combs, which filter the sea water for krill (plankton and small shellfish), its staple diet.

Most marine mammals are great travellers. In summer, the *humpback* is usually found in the cold northern seas, from Norway to Newfoundland. In winter it returns to the warm waters of Central and South America to breed off Hawaii, in the Caribbean, and round the Marianas. It's at this time that the whales' song is most likely to be heard. It can resemble the bellowing of a stag, an opera aria or even a nightingale's serenade. Lasting some ten to thirty minutes, it's audible several kilometres away.

On its long voyages, the whale maintains a cruising speed of 2–6 km/h. When hunting or if it—or its calf—is attacked, it can reach almost 25 km/h!

In spite of its 30 tonnes, the whale is extremely agile, playful and a great show-off. It can rear up vertically to look around (this is called 'spy-hopping'), leap out of the water (this is called 'breaching'), sometimes shaking its fins, and will lash the water violently with its tail, splashing all and sundry!

Like the *baleen whale*, the *sperm whale* and the *narwhal* travel the oceans from north to south, but their route remains a mystery.

Forget the mythical unicorn: its horn is nothing more than the upper left canine of the male *narwhal*, which can grow to 2.5 m!

Sharing the Oceans

In the cold seas of the Antarctic, *Adélie penguins* enjoy an extraordinary playground. In groups called packs, they jump, climb and slide on the ice floes before diving into the water.

Fish and marine mammals share the world's waters with other animals, such as reptiles (for example, turtles), birds (for example, penguins) and even mammals that are primarily land-dwellers (for example, otters).

The *leatherback* is the biggest of the turtle family, measuring 1.90 m in length and weighing on average 400 kg. With its front legs outspread, it spans 2.70 m! A solitary creature, the leatherback tirelessly journeys thousands of kilometres across the world's seas. The female returns to land every two years, where she lays a hundred or so eggs in a single night.

The *Adélie penguin* lives in the Antarctic. Every year it returns to the same beach to lay its eggs and raise its two chicks which struggle to be first served when the adults bring home fish. When small, they feed on a pap of krill which their parents regurgitate. From their twentieth day, they are gathered in huge nurseries of several thousand chicks. As they grow, they begin to eat fish and small squid.

Sea otters prefer the sunny coasts of California. Although land mammals, they spend their whole life in water, most of the time just floating on their backs. They eat, give birth and sleep in the water (they sleep rolled up in weed so the current doesn't carry them away).

The *killer whale* is a formidable hunter. It takes advantage of big waves to hurl itself on to the beach and snatch a sea-lion.

Hibernation, Aestivation and Extended Sleep

On the snow-covered ice floes, large male *polar bears* don't hibernate. They simply lie down on the bare ice and nap, protected by their thick fur and almost 10 cm of fat beneath their skin.

Ice and snow make winter a very difficult season for animals. They have to protect themselves from the cold and, above all, they need to find food.

Some animals, such as the *dormouse* and the *marmot*, 'choose' to hibernate. In September, they gorge themselves on grains, grass and fruit, accumulating as much fat as possible to make a food reserve. Sheltered safely in nests or burrows, they sleep deeply and continuously from October to April. Their heart rhythm slows down and their breathing drops to almost 1 per cent of its normal rate. They wake up very thin, but ready for the return of spring.

Other animals have a different way of beating cold and hunger. To reduce their calorie expenditure and hence their food requirements they simply sleep longer, keeping all activity to a minimum.

The *polar bear*, for example, hollows out a kind of igloo in a snowdrift, while the *red squirrel* insulates his drey with moss and dry grass. Though they all settle down to sleep as long as possible, they have regular periods when they warm themselves up and perhaps eat and drink. These may be testing times for the squirrel's memory—will it be able to find all the caches of seeds and nuts it created before going to sleep?

In summer, to protect themselves from the searing heat, many amphibians and snails cease all activity and sink into a prolonged sleep. This is called 'aestivation'.

Sleep Patterns

Where could be nicer for a siesta than a sandy beach? The *elephant seal* rests like this a great deal of the day between excursions into the water to look for food and occasional attempts to acquire a female.

All animals sleep, whether alone or in groups: this is an important function of life. But times vary between species—some are 'diurnal', sleeping at night, others 'nocturnal' and rest during the day.

On the beach, the *elephant seal* is safe—there are no other animals to threaten it, so it can rest all day and night without fear. It doesn't even need to make a bed, being quite happy to sleep on the bare ground. But this is not the case for all animals.

Every evening, the *chimpanzee* builds itself a shelter of branches and leaves in a tree. The young are excused this chore and allowed to share their mother's bed. Like humans, the great apes sleep about eight hours a night.

Sleep patterns are often influenced by an animal's predators. Whereas herbivores (such as the *zebra*, *gnu* and *Thomson's gazelle*) sleep three hours a night—mostly on their feet so they can flee at the least sign of danger—*lions* and *leopards* can afford up to 10 hours rest, settled comfortably and safely in the shade.

There are some animals with rather odd sleeping habits. For example, in the tundra, the *swan* spends the night huddled under the snow. More surprisingly, perhaps, the *swift* sleeps only a few minutes a day—and then while flying! The *bat*, on the other hand, rests hanging upside down from a beam or the walls and roofs of caves.

The *sloth* (also known as the ai or unau) must surely owe its name to the twenty hours it sleeps every day!

Fair Shares?

When the *great white shark* is hunting fish, it sometimes encounters a seal. Will the latter manage to escape?

Animals frequently share a meal, but not always by design. When a *shark* has caught its prey, for example, its companions will gather round it in the hope of sharing the feast. There won't be a fight: there's just enough for the strongest and smartest. No shark intentionally shares its food; if it can wolf down its catch in one go without leaving anything for the others, it will certainly do so!

On the African savannah, there's a strict pecking order at meal times. Irrespective of which animal caught the prey, each one receives its share of food in turn, clan by clan and starting in each case with the strongest.

So when a *lioness* catches a *gnu*, it's the males in the pride who help themselves first. The lionesses and their *cubs* must wait.

The great share-out now begins. The *hyenas* wait until the cats have finished to snatch a few morsels. Next come the *jackals*—they make do with what the hyenas have left. That's not the end of it, though: it's the *vultures'* turn to tear off the last shreds of skin. One of them, the *lammergeier* or *bearded vulture*, even flies away with the bones—it then drops them to the ground, breaking them open to reveal the marrow.

Finally, once the insects have had their share, all traces of the carcass will have disappeared.

The *great frigate-bird* has devised an ingenious method of feeding: in mid-flight, it steals the fish caught by other birds.

Hunting Techniques

With an expert swipe of its great paw, a *grizzly bear* (*brown bear*), catches a salmon in mid-air. When everyone is out fishing, the best spots will be occupied by the dominant and older bears.

Animals adopt various techniques for getting a meal, depending on the intended prey: ambushes, surprise attacks, chases, beating through the undergrowth, looting, etc.

Pelicans have a very peculiar way of fishing. Ten or so get together in shallow water, where they swim in a tight semi-circle. When they spot a shoal of fish, they all simultaneously plunge their beaks into the water and withdraw them. The pouches under their beaks (the gular pouch) serve as nets! They swallow their share of the catch, and the ballet-like routine starts all over again. The pelican chicks are now able to thrust their heads into their parents' bills to eat regurgitated pap and small fish.

The *brown bear* is a loner who can adapt to any situation; it eats whatever it finds on its wanderings. After fishing, it delicately picks a fruit or a berry before savouring it. Sometimes it will scratch at the ground, expose a nest of field mice, and eat the entire family. If it finds a hive, it licks out the honey with no fear of being stung by the angry *bees*, protected by its long, thick coat. And if hunger leads a brown bear to a sheep-fold, it will break down the gate and carry off a *ewe* or a *lamb*.

The *anteater*, as its name suggests, feeds solely on ants. It catches them with its narrow sticky tongue, which is almost 60 cm long!

Win Some, Lose Some!

The *Adélie penguin*, like the *king penguin*, feeds mainly on fish and small squid. In the breeding season, the males and females take turns to incubate the eggs and bring their catch to the chicks.

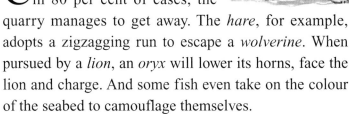

Catching prey is not easy and, in 80 per cent of cases, the quarry manages to get away. The *hare*, for example, adopts a zigzagging run to escape a *wolverine*. When pursued by a *lion*, an *oryx* will lower its horns, face the lion and charge. And some fish even take on the colour of the seabed to camouflage themselves.

For the *penguins* in the waters of Antarctica, life is much easier: when a shoal of fish arrives on their doorstep, they simply help themselves to a picnic!

On the other side of the world, in the Arctic, life's not so easy for the *Arctic fox*. Often, it has to make do with a few mouthfuls of seal stolen from a bear. So when it has the opportunity to catch a *ptarmigan* or a *variable hare*, it will devour it whole, at one sitting. If prey are numerous—for example, when there's an abundance of *lemmings*—it sets up a larder; it buries several of these small rodents in the ice—using it like a refrigerator—in the hope it will find them again if food becomes scarce. Because the *wolverine* does the same with its prey, however, the Arctic fox often uncovers a wolverine's stores, and vice versa. So the smarter of the two will enjoy the best dinners!

When the *shrike* catches too much prey, it stores the surplus by impaling it on long thorns or the spikes of barbed wire.

Tools

To drink, the *orang-utan* uses its hand as a scoop. This is one of the rare occasions it will venture into water, which it detests. When it rains, therefore, it uses a big leaf as an umbrella so it won't get wet.

Like the *orang-utan*, all the great apes use tools, chiefly to obtain food. The *chimpanzee* breaks off a thin branch from a tree and carefully peels away the leaves. This it coats with saliva and pokes into a termite mound; insects stick to it, and the chimpanzee pulls it out again and eats them. Again, leaves are very useful for drinking river water. The chimpanzee either uses one leaf like a spoon or chews up several together to make a compact ball that will act as a sponge; he soaks up water with it and then squeezes it out into his mouth.

But apes are not the only animals to use tools. The *sea otter* mostly feeds on shellfish. An expert at floating on its back, it uses its stomach as a kitchen table on which to break open shells with the aid of a small pebble.

Birds are also inventive: the *Egyptian vulture* (a small, white variety) will take a stone in its beak and use it to crack open an ostrich egg. If the stone proves too small to break the shell, it chooses a bigger one and starts again. It will continue to try out stones until it finds one big enough to do the job. Similarly, when a crow's beak isn't strong enough to open an egg, it will throw it down on to a hard surface.

The *song thrush* uses a flat stone as an anvil on which to shatter the shells of *snails*.

Varying the Menu

Whatever the weather, the *polar bear* patrols the ice in search of food. Best of all, it hopes to find a hole in the ice where the *seals* come up for air. However, it will need to be very patient and cunning to catch one.

A predator's food depends on its habitat, the climate, the season and, of course, the number of available prey in its territory. A winter that's too cold and snowy, an extra-hot summer, a fire or flood, can all upset the ecological balance and thus put an animal's life in jeopardy.

The *polar bear* is omnivorous—it eats whatever it can find. So, when food is scarce, it turns it attention from seals and varies its menu: its first choice is birds and their eggs, then *lemmings* and *variable hares*. For dessert, it will pluck a few leaves and berries. Unfortunately, no matter what the season, it's become increasingly inclined in recent years to visit both the numerous scientific bases established on its territory and the scattered native settlements, where it scavenges the refuse.

Like the polar bear, the *red fox* also rings the changes. Although *rabbits* and small rodents make up the bulk of its food, its menu is extraordinarily varied. For instance, it takes advantage of the morning dew to gorge itself on *earthworms* and, in the autumn, frequents vineyards where it feasts on the ripened grapes. On the coast, it raids the nests of sea birds, swallowing their eggs and gobbling their chicks. Whatever the conditions, it always manages to find something.

With the arrival of snow, prey becomes scarce. The *variable hare* will now find it harder to escape the pursuit of a determined and hungry *lynx*.

The Rainy Season

After months of scorching heat resulting in a shortage of grass and, above all, water, *zebras* appreciate the arrival of the rains on the African savannah.

On the African savannah, the rainy season begins in November, though at first the storms produce only a few drops. The rain brings new life, but there's also the threat of fire. Because the grass is still dry after months of scorching heat, the lightning starts numerous blazes. The animals must now flee this inferno, and old enmities are set aside: *lions, antelopes, wild dogs* and *warthogs* can be seen fleeing side by side in their haste to avoid the flames. When the fire is over, life takes up where it left off, and once more each animal must find ways to avoid being eaten by its neighbours.

In February and March the heavy rains return. This is the time on the savannah when trees and grass turn green again. Lakes and rivers overflow, and thousands of birds swoop down on the newly created marshes to gorge themselves with fish, amphibians, insects or succulent grasses.

The rainy season is also the time when *zebras, gazelles, gnus* and other ruminants give birth. It's the most difficult period of all for the young, who are at the mercy of *lions, cheetahs* and *hyenas* with offspring of their own to feed. But Nature's arranged things well: there are plenty of young animals gambolling under the protective gaze of their parents, and it's only the weakest who will end up being eaten by the carnivores.

Sheltered by an acacia, a pair of *hartebeest* hesitate to venture out in the rain to feast on the long-awaited growth of new grass.

The Long March

Nothing can halt the migrating *gnu*: even the Mara River. In a huge cloud of dust, and accompanied by a few *zebra* and *antelope*, each year they relentlessly pursue the same paths across the savannah.

At the end of April, in the Serengeti National Park in Tanzania, the *gnu* gather. First singly, then in the uproar created by a vast herd of one and a half million individuals, they take the trail that will lead them to the Masai Mara Reserve in Kenya. This is called the Great Migration. They are following the rains, in search of fresh pasture. Driven by hunger, they travel more than 700 km until, in June, they once more reach their favourite grazing: vegetation known as Sudan grass.

On this long journey, the gnu are accompanied by about 300,000 *gazelles*, 200,000 *zebra* and perhaps 10,000 *eland*.

Year after year they take the same paths, ploughing furrows across the African plain. This last, big, animal migration is especially dangerous. Of the young under one year of age, only one in ten will reach its destination. Several hundred adults will also die: from exhaustion and attacks by big cats or caught in the trap of the Mara River, which awaits them at the end of their journey. Crossing this river is a nightmare. The gnu trample over each other, disappear into the muddy, turbulent waters and—worst of all—are ambushed by armies of Nile crocodiles, who wreak havoc among the weakened animals.

The *leopard* makes the most of the *gnus'* long march. Lying in wait by river crossings, it pounces on the weakest animals.

In the Desert

The *giraffe* lives on the African savannah, where it feeds mainly on acacia leaves.

Deserts present extremely testing living conditions, from the lack of water and intense heat of Africa's Sahara to the wind and cold of the Gobi Desert in Central Asia. To survive in such places, animals have had to adapt to the harsh conditions.

The indefatigable *addax* (an antelope) ceaselessly treks the sands of the Sahara searching for the next tuft of grass. To protect itself from the sun's rays, its coat, grey in winter, turns completely white in summer. It can survive for several months without drinking, making do with moisture extracted from occasional grasses in the desert. Its stomach, however, has a reserve of several litres of water, which it can draw on as a last resort.

In the Gobi Desert, temperatures rise to 40 ºC in summer, but drop in winter to –30 ºC. All year round the wind blows at storm force. This is the habitat of the *saiga antelope*, an animal with a long, bulbous nose enabling it to filter the air it breathes, thus protecting its lungs from the bitter, snow-laden winds and burning dust storms. Its short, dense coat insulates it, summer and winter, from variations in temperature.

In the Sonora Desert in the southwestern United States, there is a curious bird called the *road-runner* that just runs and runs!

Cold and Snow

The female *Japanese macaque* gives birth to just one baby at a time. At birth, it weighs a mere 500 g. To protect itself from the cold and snow, it snuggles up against its parents.

Animals' natural environment can be hospitable or harsh. Climate (e.g. cold or snow) is only one thing they have to adapt to: various other factors are involved.

In Japan, on the island of Honshu at an altitude of 1,500 m, the temperature drops to –20 °C in winter. It's here, among other places, that the *Japanese macaque* lives. Its long, thick fur protects it from the cold and snow. Especially, though, it takes advantage of the natural hot-water springs, which are at a constant temperature of 40–60 °C. It enjoys invigorating baths and then dries itself off sitting on the surrounding hot stones.

In the high peaks of the west coast of the United States lives the *Rocky Mountain goat*. This goat may be seen at an altitude of 4000 m gambolling on rock faces with a 50-degree slope. To help it keep its grip, it has short, sturdy legs and hooves that are split into two, with a V-shaped opening at the front acting like a pair of pincers. Their hooves are also pointed to provide anchorage, with rough, non-slip undersides. In winter when the temperature plummets to –40 °C, this goat sleeps in the snow to protect itself from the cold! The snow insulates its body by trapping body heat, maintaining an average body temperature of –7 °C.

The high peaks of the Himalayas are the realm of the *snow leopard*. In summer it will venture to a height of 6,000 m in search of fresh food.

Birth in the Antarctic

It is springtime on South Georgia, and the young *king penguins* are moulting. Their thick, brown, baby down is replaced by the elegant black, white, orange and grey-blue tunic of the adult bird.

The cold not only makes it hard to find food and keep warm, but also presents problems at breeding time; on the Antarctic ice, giving birth and raising young are undertakings fraught with peril.

The *king penguin* doesn't build a nest. Instead, the female lays a single egg. She protects it from the cold by draping her brood pouch over it. About every two weeks, the parents swap places to care for the egg. This changeover, however, is fraught with dangers. The egg is fragile, and it has to be kept at the same temperature throughout the incubation period.

When the chick has hatched, the parents also take turns to feed it. Force-fed with fish and krill, it's soon big enough to join its fellows. At this stage of their development, all the chicks are gathered together in a huge group known as a nursery. This allows both parents to concentrate on feeding their offspring: the chick must lay down as large a food reserve as possible because they are only fed around once a month during the winter.

After this winter lean period, the chick is fed by its parents until it moults. When it has acquired its adult plumage, which is shortly before its first birthday, it's able to hunt for itself in the sea.

Free at last of their chick, the parents take advantage of the available food. They must eat as much as possible before returning to land to moult, often increasing their body weight from 12 to 20 kg. This reserve is vital: the moult consumes a lot of energy and the birds must moult regularly to renew their plumage and keep it waterproof and insulating.

Resembling a little leaping imp, the *Rock-hopper penguin*, with its punk haircut, is conspicuous on the Antarctic ice.

Why?

In spite of attempts to protect it in the wild, the *giant panda's* future is still very uncertain. Its low rate of reproduction and the destruction of its habitat are the main causes of its decline.

Humans do not seem to respect nature. Our ill-considered exploitation of natural resources and our disregard of the environment are leading to a disaster. The forest is the most dramatic example of this: every day another species is threatened with extinction as a result of deforestation—insects, flowers, birds and, more sensationally, all the great apes.

Every day, thousands of tonnes of pesticides are sprayed on to our planet. In France, for instance, the house martin population has dropped by more than 80 per cent in less than 10 years as a result of the disappearance of the insects they feed on and the destruction of their nests: they deface the walls of our houses!

Every day, tonnes of plastic refuse and thousands of litres of hydrocarbons are dumped in the sea. Turtles suffocate when they swallow plastic bags in mistake for jellyfish; oil slicks devastate our beaches and bring death to sea birds.

Every day, human beings in their folly slaughter animals for no reason. For example, because the rhinoceros is now a protected species, traditional Asian pharmacies have to make do with the horns of the male saiga instead. Today, only 1 male remains for each 100 females, and the global population has diminished by 90 per cent!

The *Tasmanian wolf*—the last great carnivorous marsupial—disappeared for ever at the beginning of the twentieth century.

How Can We Help?

It was thought the *koala* was safe because its numbers appeared to be increasing. But disease has decimated its population. Add to this the destruction of its habitat and, once again, its future is uncertain.

Throughout the world there are National Parks, wildlife parks and conservation areas. Associations dedicated to protecting wildlife are springing up all over the place. In animal reserves and the wild, there are programmes to protect and reintroduce endangered species. Without them, what would have happened to the koala, the nene goose, Père David's deer, the African elephant or the Arabian oryx? Saving animals and their environment isn't, however, just a job for the experts: it's a responsibility we all share.

What can we—ordinary people—do, therefore, on a day-to-day basis to preserve the environment and to protect existing species?

Perhaps, quite simply, we should rediscover respect: we should acknowledge, as Antoine de Saint-Exupéry put it, that the world does not belong to us—that we merely hold it in trust for future generations. This means realising that every time an animal disappears, a little bit of ourselves is lost. It means being prepared, every day, to give up a few more of our creature comforts to conserve the world's natural resources—particularly water and timber. It means swapping our guns for cameras. It means laying aside our fear of the wild, the unknown and the different.

One of the most touching success stories of recent years has been the reintroduction of a herd of *Przewalski horses*. These horses now run freely across the plains of Mongolia.